INCENSE

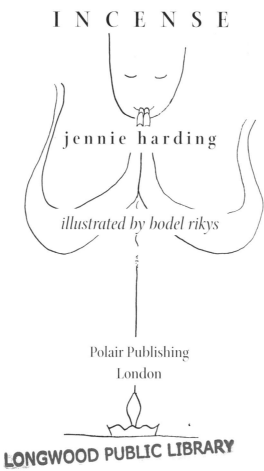

jennie harding

illustrated by bodel rikys

Polair Publishing
London

LONGWOOD PUBLIC LIBRARY

First published October 2005

© Jennie Harding, 2005
Drawings © Bodel Rikys, 2005

British Library Cataloguing-in-Publication Data
A catalogue record for this book is available from the British Library

ISBN 0-9545389-7-8

Acknowledgments
Warm and grateful thanks to Colum Hayward for his patience and gentle guardianship during this project.
Also warm thanks to my dear friends Ann and Ray Burger for providing—yet again—a peaceful place for me to write.

Set in Arepo at the Publishers
and printed in Great Britain by Cambridge University Press

CONTENTS

A Lavender Field

INTRODUCTION: THE SCENT OF INCENSE

IT IS LATE summer, and I am working in my garden. I am cutting back some very bushy aromatic shrubs which have produced masses of leaves and twigs over the warm season, and also trimming lots of lavender bushes which have finished flowering. As I work, my nose is filled with pungent aromas, herbal scents, green and fragrant perfumes from these plants. In the end I have collected several large heaps of material.

I am not going to throw this mass of leaves, stalks and flowers away. I save it carefully in bunches, stored in large bags in my shed, to dry slowly over the next few months. Then on New Year's Eve I make a fire, starting with the woodier branches, adding more of the dried plants as it crackles and burns. Immediately, the air is filled with the aromatic pungent smoke of the plants, the remembrance of summer, the old aspects of the year burning away to create the spark for a new time, a new beginning. The smoke purifies the air, it cleanses away negativity, and my friends and I gather together around this fire quietly to release the old year and welcome the new. The smoke is our incense, made from plants that grow around us. We breathe in its aroma, our minds are stilled, our hearts at peace. Incense creates an inner space that allows us to connect with deeper aspects of ourselves, to be clear and filled with a new sense of purpose.

People have been burning aromatic plants, resins and flowers as incense for thousands of years. No-one knows exactly when this began. Humankind has a long silent pre-history, before the advent of civilizations and writing, where for millennia we wandered the surface of the planet, collecting and gathering the materials we needed to live. Part of that hunter–gatherer activity involved the testing, trying and use of many different plants for food, medicine and ritual. For thousands of years, medicine men and women, ancient practitioners of shamanism, the oldest spiritual tradition on Earth, used aromatic smoke for journeys into the spirit world to help the sick. As we shall discover, these scents—chemical ingredients in the plants—have special effects on the mind and senses, and were deliberately chosen for such ritual use. Since less than five per cent of the Earth's plant species are aromatic, these rare plants must have been considered very special when they were found. Many of these plant species are still around today, often growing in the lands where they were first venerated. From early human beginnings, as civilizations grew, aromatic plants, spices and resins were burned as part of sacred rituals, often associated with different deities, offered as precious symbols of devotion. Even now, this practice continues all over the world.

In the West, incense is often associated with Roman Catholic rituals or with cheap Indian joss-sticks and hippies, but this is a narrow perspective. Thanks to Eastern influences in the past decades, there has been a renewal of interest in the appreciation and use of quality incense for personal applications, for example to clear space for meditation or quiet thinking, to make an environment welcoming, or to celebrate a special event. This is the terrain we shall cover in this book.

We shall take a look at incense traditions from around the world and see what we can learn from them. Taking a journey through some of the most fabulous and ancient cultures on the planet we shall delve into over 5000 years of aromatic history. We will find out more about some special plants which are used as ingredients in incense combinations: some from exotic, faraway places and some which are found much closer to home. You will find out how to make your own incense blends, how to burn them safely and how to use them to enhance the journey of your life. You will want to create your own ceremonies to mark the passage of time, to celebrate life events, or use the aroma of incense to feel relaxed and restored.

As you begin your journey into the world of incense, you may well find your sense of your inner self begins to grow. This effect has been experienced by your ancestors across time. Incense is seen by many cultures as a symbol of connection between humans, the earth, the air, the sky and the stars: as a way from the visible to the invisible. The smoke itself is the path; you have only to watch a stick of fragrant incense burning and you see a kind of spiral pattern rising upwards. This pattern is reflected in paintings, art and hieroglyphs from many cultures where smoke is seen as a message. Burning incense and sacred herbs is far more significant than simple room-fragrancing; it is an intentional act of importance. By exploring what this means in different cultures we can then use it ourselves and discover how to bring a sense of the sacred into our everyday lives.

Why is this important? Because it is a deep instinct within us, despite the whirl of modern life. More and more people are beginning to seek ways to have a deeper connection with the sacred, with nature, in order to relieve feelings of isolation and disconnectedness which technology cannot satisfy. We are still connected to our ancestral roots: to those groups of humans who wandered and moved with the seasons, who interacted directly with the diverse wonders of Creation. When we stand around the sacred fire, or inhale the scented smoke of aromatic plants, we stand with them.

Both 'new age' and traditional ecclesiastical shops sell charcoal shaped to take incense. When it comes to obtaining aromatic materials to make incense, it is wonderful to grow, pick and dry your own herbs as far as possible. Rarer ingredients like woods and resins need to be obtained from good herbal suppliers. The following websites are good points of contact for further information:

UK: www.herbsociety.org.uk
USA: www.herbalgram.org
AUS: www.focusonherbs.com.au.

CHAPTER 1
AROMATIC BEGINNINGS

S WE ARE going to explore the world of incense, it helps to begin by understanding how the sense of smell works. Of course we know that we detect hundreds of aromas every day; but for most of us, this sense is rather a mystery. Often we only notice it when it is absent, for example when we have a blocked nose because of a cold. Then suddenly the world seems remote: food has no taste, we feel cut off from everything. When the sense of smell returns, it is as if life goes from black and white back into colour. Our appetite returns, we feel better. Certain smells attract our attention very easily, such as the aroma of baking or the perfume of a rose. If we are observant, we might notice how those aromas affect us, making us feel hungry or changing our mood so that we smile. What is actually happening?

When you breathe in, microscopic aromatic particles pass up your nostrils in swarms, warmed and literally excited by the air in the coiling passageways of your nostrils. At the very back of your nose,

behind the main bone called the septum, there are some patches of very special cells. These have minuscule tendrils which wave in the air like tiny sea anemones, capturing the aromatic particles. The action triggers nerve-impulses that flash via connecting points straight into your brain. The entire process takes less than two seconds; these special 'smell cells' are considered to be the closest brain cells to the outside world.

Once smell-impulses reach the brain, they are interpreted in many different ways, depending on the paths they take. Research into the sense of smell points to two general types of reaction.

First, deep within the core of the brain is an area called the *rhinencephalon*—literally 'smell brain'— where there are anatomical structures that have been there throughout our human evolution. These centres are sometimes also called the 'old brain'. If you react to a smell here, your reactions will be non-verbal, mostly via facial expressions of like or dislike, body movements towards or away from the aroma, and other reactions like increase in saliva or stomach growlings if this aroma means food. You might make a sound like 'ahh' or 'mm' or an expression of dislike. This area is also linked to early memories and feelings, which can be strong, instinctive: a 'gut' response.

Second, we have the 'grey matter' that sits over the older brain area, where we experience so-called 'higher brain' functions like rational thinking, creativity and leaps of thinking, processing and problem solving. These areas link to speech centres, so we evaluate verbally what we are experiencing—'Oh, that reminds me of ... '. Aromas experienced here can induce states of excitement, inspiration or mood enhancement, with advanced expression through words or other creative activity.

So the higher brain area is where we evaluate and express complex feelings and emotions; the old brain area relates to strong gut instincts that are beyond words. Both aspects of the brain are highly affected by the sense of smell. It can be interesting to monitor your own responses to smells for a while—do you just react, or do you notice simple emotions, or do you want to express how you feel in a more complex way? This can give you clues as to how aromas are affecting you and why.

Fragrances and aromas of plants have the capacity to excite us, to take us to places of deep memory, as well as to influence our moods—whether we are relaxed, stimulated, excited or inspired. Inhaling a fragrance can often have an immediate effect on behaviour, stopping us in our tracks, changing the pattern of the moment. In this we are no different from our distant ancestors. Archaeological and present-day studies of ethnic cultures, people who still live close to their natural environment, suggest that our ancestors clearly relied much more on their sense of smell than we do. It was not simply a matter of finding food and medicine—there was also the need to detect animals to hunt by picking up their odour trails, or to recognize scents of predators who might attack humans. Odour research shows that some of our most instinctive responses to smells are still responses to scents of animal origin—like musk, for example, even if we have never actually pursued a deer. Early humans lived in a world where their sense of smell was one of the keenest ways to interact with their environment, both seen and unseen.

Some of the earliest ingredients of incense are fragrant woods and resins that may well have been discovered by accident, placing them on a fire and noticing the effects of their scented smoke. By the time of the earliest recorded civilizations, these ingredients were in heavy use, not just burned as incense but also used in sacred buildings. One of the first known instances occurred when the Old Testament's King Solomon commanded that his temple should have inner pillars made of trunks of cedars of Lebanon. Reddish cedarwood, even before burning, is intensely aromatic, and would have imparted a fine, deep incense-like aroma to the whole of the interior of the building. To be able to command such a quantity of aromatic wood was a sign of Solomon's power and wealth, but clearly the role of the perfume of cedarwood was highly special and significant too—creating the right atmosphere in the temple for worship.

The ancient Egyptians had a huge appetite for incense made from resin—and what they prized more than anything was frankincense. This name is from old French, *franc encens*—meaning 'true incense'; another name for it is olibanum, which some writers think means 'oil of Lebanon' but could also be linked to the Hebrew word *lebonah* which is a word for incense.* This amazing shrub grows in the deserts of the Middle East, in what is now Oman

*The word 'incense' itself comes from the Latin *incendere*, to set alight.

and Somalia in Africa; the resin is produced by the plant as a response to trauma. If there is a cut or tear in the bark, the tree makes 'tears' of resin to seal it, most likely to prevent moisture loss. For millennia, people have collected the pieces of dried, hardened and highly aromatic resin, sometimes making deliberate cuts in the bark to encourage the bushes to produce more. To this day, the collection and transport of frankincense to market is a well-guarded business, still using the 'incense route' from Arabia and Africa. This brought precious pieces of frankincense resin to Egyptian potentates over 5000 years ago. Then and now, large caravans of traders brought it up through Ethiopia to the kingdom of Egypt, from where it was traded across the whole Mediterranean basin.

In ancient Egypt, frankincense was a main ingredient in sacred offerings to the gods and to the Pharaoh, seen as a representation of godhead on earth. By about 3000 BCE, there was even a special office in the royal household created just to keep track of supplies. Incense was offered in a number of ways; one was by waving a small handheld censer, an incense holder made of mood and metal which allowed a hot coal and incense to be safely carried. Handheld pots also appear on temple carvings and paintings, as well as many representations of incense burning directly on altars. Records show that Pharaoh Rameses III used over a million jars of frankincense in his thirty-year reign—a staggering amount. Daily offerings of frankincense were made to statues of the gods in ancient Egyptian temples, and it was a key ingredient in embalming processes. As well as being used alone, it was also a key ingredient in many combinations of aromatic ingredients for perfumes, remedies and medicines.

So why was frankincense so attractive—then and now? The aroma of the smoke from burning granules of resin is regarded as dry, pungent, with slightly musky elements in it as well as woody notes. Odour researchers have suggested that these musky notes are significant; they are chemically very similar to elements in human and animal odour secretions, particularly the sex hormones. Indeed, many of the most common and ancient incense sources like cedarwood, spikenard, sandalwood, myrrh and frankincense share this characteristic. It is likely that human beings have been drawn to them, possibly subconsciously, out of a deep instinctive response to something with a scent reminiscent of our own—bringing mysterious feelings of ecstasy and release into other levels of consciousness. These aromatics are evocative and powerful in their effects

because they trigger such deeply sensitive responses within the brain; in large quantities, the effect can be very emotive. Over millennia, humankind has been drawn to these special fragrances because they arouse feelings and open the heart. In addition, scientific studies have shown that inhalation of these types of aroma also induces certain physical reactions; blood pressure is lowered, breathing slows and brainwaves settle into a meditative pattern. This may be why they were constantly selected for religious purposes, so as to allow large numbers of people to participate in rituals, as well as enhancing the receptivity of the priesthood during ceremonies.

Ancient Egyptian healing practices also used the ritual inhalation of incense. At the temple of Osiris at Abydos on the Nile, patients who consulted the priest-healers were conducted to underground chambers where they would sleep while incense permeated the room where they lay. This was regarded as a key way to unlock their dreams, which the priests would interpret the following day and thus—hopefully—find their cure. Smells do affect us when we are asleep, and some aromas—such as some species of sage—are known to bring about colourful dreams! To this day in shamanic practice all over the world, in countries like Africa, Peru, and Tibet, the shaman or medicine man still deliberately spreads aromatic smoke over his patient to reach the dream world, the space beyond the visible, to dream or intuit what is needed for their healing. The aromas and the smoke together are the vital link with the unseen; the brain is affected by the scents used, and unlocks different states of consciousness.

Perhaps the idea of aromas triggering different levels of consciousness is startling and somewhat challenging, but maybe your concept of what is 'real' could be stretched a little. People in other cultures throughout history have accepted quite readily that 'reality' is complex, more like a series of ripples on a pool than simply what you see when you wake up in the morning. In the West, we have become very linear in our thinking; connecting with incense traditions reminds us that to some other humans, 'life' is made up of many worlds which interlink with each other, the worlds of seen and unseen, physical and non-physical, matter and energy. The sense of smell is intriguing because it is not as obviously 'physical' as seeing with the eyes or hearing with the ears; smell has sometimes been called the 'silent sense', it is seen as more subtle, more mysterious. Perhaps this is why it is at the root of so many ancient traditions that use aromas to reach the spirit world.

At a Hong Kong Temple

CHAPTER 2
A WONDERFUL AROMATIC JOURNEY

LET US now embark on a magical journey through some of the most important incense traditions of the world. This is an exotic and wide-reaching exploration, taking us far and wide. Time and time again you will realize how deeply embedded incense traditions are within different cultures and civilizations. This trail shows how humankind's relationship with key incense ingredients is long-lived, stretching far back to the first written records, yet still continuing today; incense is a key link to lineage, heritage and deeply-held spiritual beliefs.

India and Tibet

The whole Indian subcontinent is a vast source of naturally-occurring incense ingredients. These range from exotic flowers like lotus, rose and jasmine to precious woods like sandalwood, as well as spices like cinnamon and cassia, leaves such as patchouli and roots like vetiver, ginger or spikenard. In ancient India, incense was made out of combinations of all of these ingredients, as well as imported ingredients like frankincense. Exotic ingredients such as extracts of true musk, civet and ambergris were obtained from different animal species as well, and combined with plant extracts in special formulae closely guarded by different rival families. Vast quantities of incense powders, tablets and pastes were made for use in daily ritual as well as for religious ceremonies; the tradition of Indian incense-making stretches back at least five thousand years, and continues today. The more familiar Indian incense sticks (*agarbatties*) are a modern invention of the nineteenth and twentieth centuries, where incense paste is hand-rolled around a thin twig; in ancient times powder was more often used directly, sprinkled onto hot coals.

The Indian spiritual tradition takes in the worship of countless deities, and each of them commanded a special incense blend. Many deities had specific links to particular plants. For example, the god of perfume, Indra, was always anointed with sandalwood oil on the breast; while the god of love, Kama, carried an arrow tipped with jasmine. No incense for holy worship could contain less than eight ingredients, and most contained many more. Typical key ingredients were sandalwood, camphor, vetiver, costus or saffron.

Incense use arose out of the depths of Indian spiritual belief in the divine elements of Creation, the five elements of earth (*bhumi*), air (*wayu*) fire (*ag*) water (*nir*) and ether (*gaggan*), activated by the power of the Source to give life. Ancient Indian belief rested on the notion of the offering, the burning of sacred incense as a symbol of thanks and veneration for the abundance of Creation. The mind- and heart-opening effects of the glorious scents of flowers, woods and spices was in effect a way of experiencing the power of spirit. So even to this day, temples are still cleansed on a daily basis, the statues washed and anointed with oil, hung with scented garlands of beautiful flowers like jasmine, and bathed in the sacred smoke of incense offerings. In ancient times, *rishis*, Indian wise men, lived lives of dedicated service to their people; part of their work was to understand all the plants which were native to their

region. They were responsible for creating purifying and healing combinations of plant ingredients for ceremonial incense. Some ceremonies involved large numbers of people—even whole communities; these were called *yagnas* and were performed at times when the seasons changed. Then very specially-shaped fire pits were dug and incense burned on a vast scale to cleanse and purify the spirits of all members of the community.

In addition, the sacred medicine of India, the ancient and revered tradition of Ayurveda, the 'science of life', relied upon aromatic ingredients used directly on and around a person to reawaken spiritual fire, and ignite the dynamics of healing. Since everything is made up of the five sacred elements, using the correct combinations of aromatic ingredients in massage, baths and inhalation of incense is a highly-effective treatment for the individual. This traditional and ancient form of medicine is still practised in India and around the world today. One of the most important roles of incense burning was to slow and deepen the breathing; since in Ayurveda, the breath is the source of life, not just the inhalation of oxygen but also the intake of *prana*, actual life-force, into the body, then improving the rate and depth of the breath, was a key element in healing practice.

One of the finest Indian incense masala or mixtures you can buy in stick form is called 'Nag Champa' incense. It is one of the most pure blends, and contains no synthetic ingredients like many cheaper incense brands. It has a beautiful woody and resiny aroma, soft and not too sweet, and it is an excellent incense to use to purify your space for meditation or quiet time. It is usually available from health food stores and New Age shops. There is also another range of pure incense blends called 'Auroville' incenses, made in the ashram communities of Sri Aurobindo, a famous Indian guru or teacher. Here there are many to choose from, and you need to be guided by your own sense of smell.

In Tibet, the use of incense is also absolutely fundamental to worship and traditional medicine. The wood of the Himalayan cedar, *Cedrus deodora*, imparts a key fragrance element here—deep, pungent, smoky and subtle. Buddhist use of incense is designed to purify and cleanse space and prepare the mind and body for meditation. In the hills and high mountains of the Himalayas are also found other fascinating and ancient aromatic ingredients such as spikenard, the very pungent and musky root of *Nardostachys jatamansi*, which is likely to have been the unusual and very expensive fragrance in the ointment used by Mary Magdalene in the anointing of the feet of Christ. In the first century CE, the Greek physician Dioscorides noted hundreds of plants and spices which were available for medicinal use. Some, like spikenard, had clearly travelled to the Mediterranean region all the way from distant India. Even then, spice-trade routes covered thousands of miles over entire continents.

Middle East

Incense is a vital element in Arabian culture, and again this has its roots in deepest history. In the Arabian deserts of Oman and Somalia lay the native habitats of frankincense, as we have already seen, as well as other aromatic shrubs like myrrh. The name myrrh derives from the Arabic *murr* which means bitter; the taste and the aroma of myrrh have that definite quality. As a pink powder, myrrh was a key ingredient in many ancient incense recipes. Recent archaeological work has unearthed the ruins of an ancient city called Ubar in Oman, which must have been a vital point for the distribution of frankincense from the famous Dhofar valley in the south of the country, perhaps as far back as ancient Egyptian times. The Dhofari coastal plain is an important area for producing crops like coconuts, bananas and other vegetables, but it is also still the source of what many consider to be the world's best frankincense.

The use of the purifying powers of incense is a natural daily ritual in Arab countries; it is said to please God, to protect from evil spirits and to cleanse body and mind. It is the custom to burn *bokhur*, or traditional incense blends, in most Omani homes. Every village has its *bokhur* maker, an expert in the blending of incense. Typical ingredients in incense combinations include rosewater, sugar, ambergris, sandalwood, frankincense and myrrh. The incense is placed in burners made of clay, porcelain or silver, filled with hot coals. The smoke of is used to purify clothes, especially before wedding ceremonies.

The Arabs also venerate rose and jasmine as perfume and incense ingredients, and both of these plants grow extensively in their climate. A special musky-smelling precious wood called *oudh*, which is a kind of agarwood imported from Malaysia at staggering expense (at least £17,000 per kilo), is still used today in incense blends for special occasions such as weddings, christenings or funerals, and is even given as a valuable part of a woman's dowry to show wealthy status. Oudh is the most expensive incense and perfume ingredient in the world.

In Yemen, it is still the custom to buy incense as a regular part of everyday life, and incense makers are highly revered. Women anoint their skin with palm oil and then perfume themselves with the smoke of incense. It is also a custom to use incense to scent clothes, often for hours at a time. Clothes impregnated with incense are worn to weddings or other ceremonies. When a child is born, incense is used to perfume the house after the birth and also burned around the mother and child during the postnatal period to cleanse and protect them. The technique involves placing hot coals in metal censers often made of copper, so the fragrance can be spread through a house or a space. Special ingredients include carnation flowers, cardamom seeds, sandalwood, asafoetida, myrrh, frankincense and sugar.

In Jewish tradition, incense has a very vital role to play in religious rituals, and the historical roots of this lie in the Bible. The Book of Exodus, Chapter 3, contains the following description.

Then the Lord said to Moses 'Take fragrant spices, gum resin, onycha and galbanum and pure frankincense in equal amounts and make a fragrant blend of incense, the work of a perfumer.... Grind some of it to powder and place it front of the Testimony in the Tent of meeting where I will meet with you. It shall be most holy to you.'

The associations between incense and God are very clear here; it would seem that incense is almost a means of communication with God, or at least vital to the preparation of sacred space so that communication may take place. In modern Israel, efforts are being made to restore ancient Jewish rituals to a rebuilt Temple in Jerusalem. This includes the building of an altar of acacia wood on which is burned a special sacred incense blend called Ketoret, made up of a combination of ingredients found in the Talmud, the sacred writings of Judaism. These ingredients are listed as balsam, clove, galbanum, frankincense, myrrh, cassia, spikenard, saffron, costus and cinnamon. The Talmud states that three things revive a person's soul—pleasant sights, pleasant sounds and pleasant smells. It relates that women did not need to wear perfume when the Ketoret burned, because of its fine fragrance which permeated the air. The Ketoret was offered three times daily in the days of the original Temple, and it was a supreme honour to be selected as the priest in the ritual.

In the Old Testament, there is a wonderful hymn which mentions many key incense ingredients—it is the 'Song of Solomon'. Here is a brief extract;

I am the Rose of Sharon, and the lily of the valleys.... Thy plants are an orchard of pomegranates, with pleasant fruits ... camphire with spikenard ... and saffron; calamus and cinnamon with all trees of frankincense; myrrh and aloes, with all the chief spices....

Though commentators still debate the exact botanical details of some of these plants, many of them are recognizable by name, and still grow in the Middle East or were obtainable from traders via the Red Sea and Egypt. Their mention in the hymn emphasizes the precious and abundant nature of God.

Myrrh was a key ingredient in purification rituals for Hebrew women, especially for the months preceding and after childbirth. It is interesting to note that two of the key gifts brought to Jesus at his birth were frankincense and myrrh: vital precious symbols, cleansing and purifying agents, anointing and embalming ingredients, and revered incense elements, believed to have the ability to sanctify a relationship with God. They are presented on a par with gold, the metal of kings; in fact, there are numerous ancient accounts from Egypt and the Middle East of rare aromatics being regarded as comparable with gold. This is because of their rarity, the reverence with which they were treated, and the fact that only the mighty and powerful could afford them.

Europe

Most of our appreciation of the early use of aromatics and incense in Europe comes from Greek and Roman sources, for example from writers like Pliny who compiled a book called *Naturalis Historia*—his 'Natural History'—in the first century CE. He was fascinated by the aromas of flowers, in particular rose, crocus, hyacinth and violet. These kinds of scents were associated with youth, sweetness, purity and divinity—in literature, often the gods themselves were seen as announcing their imminent arrival by a burst of pure fragrance. The ancient Greeks and Romans were very fond of perfumes and incense, to fragrance the body, to enhance social occasions and to please their gods.

Because the Greek and Roman civilizations had close ties with Egypt, so many of the key aromatics we have seen like frankincense, cassia and myrrh found their way to Europe across the Mediterranean sea. Wealthy and powerful Romans scented their banquets with precious incense, floors were scattered inches deep in rose petals, and guests were served aromatic food and draped with wreaths of aromatic flowers and leaves. Thick sticky unguents, like heavy oily ointments, or powdered mixtures of incense were popular as ways of using aromatic ingredients.

The ancient Greeks and Romans also used herbs burned on hot coals as a way of purifying the air and helping to heal disease. The hot climate of the Mediterranean is full of wonderfully vigorous aromatic herbs and shrubs, such as the bay laurel, *Laurus nobilis*, whose leaves were woven into crowns for victors in battle or in Roman games. Bay leaves were also used to fumigate sickrooms to keep infection away and to cleanse the air. Other pungent herbs like rosemary, peppermint, juniper, myrtle and lavender were burned medicinally to help uplift the spirits and speed up healing.

Precious incense was also burned at funerals. The Roman emperor Nero in the first century CE gained notoriety when he burned massive quantities—priceless even by today's standards—of frankincense and other incense ingredients at the funeral of his wife Poppeia. An amusing account is preserved in the writings of the poet Martial, who describes how a runaway slave makes a living stealing aromatics from funeral pyres; 'The unguents and cassia, and myrrh that smells of funerals, and the frankincense half burned snatched from the pyre, and the cinnamon snatched from the bier of death—these, rascally Zoilus, surrender from your own pocket'. Notice how the slave is prepared to risk his own neck to gather the aromatics, clearly because they have value! Incense had double uses in funerals—it masked the odour of the body as well as placating the gods and hopefully ensuring peaceful passage to the next world. The ancient Greeks regarded their version of paradise, the Elysian fields, to be scented too; the incense burned on the funeral pyre was like the breath of heaven.

In Western Europe, incense is mostly associated with the development of the Roman Catholic and Greek Orthodox churches, which have used frankincense, storax and myrrh in particular since the early centuries of the last millennium. The use of a censer or thurible to spread incense found its way into the celebration of the Mass, particularly at the point of the Offertory, where the gifts of the congregation are offered to the High Altar. Currently, incense is used in Roman Catholic ritual at Mass, blessings, functions, precessions and choral offices. Hand censers are held away from the body at chest height and the incense swung towards the recipient with an up-and-down motion. In many great cathedrals, there are much larger censers, which swing over the entire congregation at intervals.

In the so-called Dark Ages, roughly from the sixth to the eighth centuries CE, it is likely that there were well-established systems of herbal healing in the extreme West of Europe, the British Isles and Ireland. The ancient Anglo-Saxons had herbs they regarded as sacred, especially aromatic yarrow, *Achillea millefolium*, and although very little written evidence survives from that period, some archaeologists speculate that the way they used their herbs may have been much more along the lines of shamanism: that is, by burning them on the fire and inhaling the smoke, as well as using them on the body. This is because pollen grains from the remains of ancient fires and cooking areas have turned out to be from plant species like yarrow.

The use of handheld incense burners in the West was very noticeable during the Great Plague of the seventeenth century. Men who worked as physicians at that time wore leather robes, a leather hat to cover the entire head with a beak-like projection filled with spices to purify the air they breathed, and they carried a censer to fumigate themselves, other people and the space where they walked. Although the aromatics seem to have granted a good deal of protection to these individuals, the origin of the anti-infectious properties of herbs, resins and spices does not seem to have been clearly understood.

Apart from the use of incense in a religious context, mainly in Roman Catholicism, its daily significance and importance have diminished in Western Europe over the past few hundred years. The story in the West is very different from countries like India or places like China and Japan, where incense use by ordinary people is very much a part of everyday life. This is due to aspects of Western cultural development and religious history, where swings away from ritual towards extreme simplicity have sometimes created a climate of suspicion around the use of aromatic substances. This might be because these aromas are known to be powerful!

In the nineteenth century and into the twentieth, as more and more people travelled to India and the East and came back into contact with incense in those distant cultures, so the importance of sacred scents was rediscovered. Perhaps now is a time where we have the opportunity to reconnect with and redefine our use of aromatics, so that we can once again revere them as gifts of nature.

The Americas

The story of incense in North America is dominated by the role of aromatic herbs in the rituals and sacred ceremonies of the Native American tribes. Although herbs and ingredients would vary according to the precise location on the vast North American land-mass, nevertheless the practices used and the reasons behind them were often similar. The use of these techniques has been handed down over generations and still persists today.

The most well-known application of sacred smoke is in the ceremony known as 'smudging'. This is where combinations of sacred herbs are burned in a small holder, and, with the use of a feather, the smoke is brushed over and all around the recipient. It can also be done to fumigate a room, to cleanse away negativity or to prepare a space for healing.

Because of the different geographical location, the herbs used for typical smudging ceremonies are native to North America. Here is a selection of the most common.

Desert Sage—*Artemisia tridentata*—is native to the USA and is very different in chemistry from the European sages (*Salvia* species). It is used to cleanse and purify negativity with a powerful effect.

Cedar—again, this refers to a particular evergreen species called *Thuja occidentalis* which botanically is completely different from the cedarwood trees of Lebanon, the Atlas mountains or the Himalayas (all *Cedrus* species). American cedar clears negative emotions.

Sweetgrass—*Hierochole odorata*—this brings back positive energy after cleansing with desert sage. It is another classic smudging herb.

White Sage—*Salvia apiana*—this type of US sage has a gentler aroma than desert sage, and is used in similar ways.

Yerba Santa—*Eriodictyon californicus*—(the name means 'sacred herb' in Spanish) this herb sanctifies and protects boundaries.

In addition to these herbs, particularly in areas of Southern USA and Mexico, there is a special tree called *Bereseru microphylla* which yields a resin called copal. This resin has been called the 'frankincense of the West'. It was sacred to the Mayan people of the Yucatan peninsula, who burned it to carry their prayers to the gods. It has a beautiful sweet yet pine-like aroma, encouraging deep and slow breathing.

The process of smudging involves placing an individual herb or a mixture into a small heatproof ceramic dish. The smudge is lit and gently fanned to life with a feather; some native traditions specify an eagle feather for the best results. Then the bowl is carried to the recipient, and starting at the left foot, the smoke is fanned up the left side of the body,

Copal

over the head, and down the back of the left side. Then the process is repeated over the right side of the body. There are many ways of performing a smudging, and some teachers suggest using your intuition. The feather is vital, because it strokes and combs the smoke through the person's individual energy field, so cleansing away any negativity.

Native American people will smudge before and after healing, or before and after a special ceremony; they regard the practice as a kind of 'spiritual hygiene', a vital and necessary cleansing to avoid any clinging negativity. Smudging can also be done before moving into a room to work, or when arriving in a new home. The possibilities are endless. The key is the intention, to allow the smoke to cleanse and purify the space, enhancing the positive energies of healing, love and the sacred awareness of spirit.

If you want to try smudging, you can buy specially-prepared smudge sticks, which are bundles of sacred herbs, from specialist suppliers by mail order, or from New Age shops. A bundle of herbs need not be burned completely in one go; you can light the end of the smudge stick and fan the smoke enough to do one smudging treatment, then snuff out the bundle in the container and leave it until next time. It is good to keep a special ceramic container especially for this purpose.

In South America, the burning of sacred herbs is part of traditional healing practices in countries like Peru or in parts of the Amazon, where the medicine man is a shaman, 'one who walks between the worlds'. Even to this day, there are still places within the rainforest where medicine men 'dream' or intuit the location of herbs they need for healing, and following the dream they simply go out and find them. Burning aromatic plants and woods like rosewood over a sick person helps to 'smoke out' negative influences and speeds up healing. The tragedy is that as more and more of the rainforest disappears, so does this incredible heritage of healing and inter-

action with the natural world beyond the 'seen'. In Peru, many of the healers are women, called 'curanderas', and they use combinations of infusions of herbs to give treatments, as well as burning herbs during consultations with patients to enhance their intuitive and diagnostic skills. Their methods can be very effective, though modern medicine has trouble understanding how; this is because western science does not generally accept the existence of the world of spirit.

China and Japan

Incense traditions in the Far East are some of the most ancient of the earth, reaching far back into known history. The Chinese have one of the oldest systems of herbal medicine in existence, and traditions involving the use of incense there are thousands of years old, linking to medicine, healing and to spiritual ceremonies. Sandalwood, a gum called storax, cassia (a type of cinnamon) and true cinnamon were common incense ingredients, combined into powders. Balls of burning jasmine were used to cleanse the air before festivals. In temples where rituals of Taoism, Confucianism and later Buddhism were conducted, constant daily cleansing and purifying of the space with incense was the norm—and still is where such temples are still found today. One of the most important incense ingredients in China was—and still is—Borneo Camphor, *Dryobalanops aromatica*, which is native to South-East Asia. The trees produce large quantities of wonderful whitish crystals of powerful smelling resin, which has a smell which is pungent, penetrating and also slightly sweet. This ingredient is extensively used in Chinese medicine, even being taken internally, and is a favourite base for Chinese incense formulae, used for embalming and funerals, but also in the making of soap! Borneo camphor is difficult to obtain in the west, and should not be confused with the more commonly available White Camphor, *Cinnamonum camphora*, which carries toxicity risks and is not safe to use in incense-making.

In Hong Kong, the burning of incense is vital to every religious ceremony, with many temples burning it constantly. Even in families, incense is burned daily to keep the family safe from one generation to the next and protect them from evil spirits; fragrant scents are believed to attract good and helpful spirits. The name of the city of Hong Kong is significant to our story—'hong' means 'fragrant' or 'incense' and 'kong' means 'harbour'. From its earliest times, the port of Hong Kong was a vital staging post in the incense trade of the Far East.

From India and China, many religious traditions and beliefs spread to Japan, especially during the sixth and seventh centuries CE. There, Buddhist traditions mingled with the already well-established spiritual practices of Shinto, and continue to co-exist today. Japan is full of countless shrines to different deities, with different forms of spiritual observance. Incense plays a vital role in making offerings. Familiar ingredients imported from China included sandalwood, spikenard, cassia, clove, frankincense and aloe wood, and to this day the precise profession of incense blending continues to be revered in Japan.

The Buddhist Tradition

According to Buddhist tradition, incense ingredients fall into five key categories. Here they are listed with examples of aromatics in each group.

Buddha family: transmutation of Ignorance—e.g Aloe wood
Vajra family: transmutation of Aversion—e.g Clove
Padma (lotus) family: transmutation of Desire—e.g Sandalwood

Ratna family: transmutation of Pride—e.g Borneo Camphor

Karma family: transmutation of Envy—e.g Turmeric.

The blending of key ingredients in delicately-balanced proportions is necessary to assist the spiritual unfoldment of an individual.

In Japan by the eleventh century CE there was an intense demand for incense; special competitions and contests were held where competitors had to guess the contents of their opponents' incense blends. To be able to judge and distinguish the subtleties of different smoky aromas was a mark of culture and spiritual attainment, practised by wealthy and high status nobility. These incense contests developed over hundreds of years into what is known as *Kodo*, the Art or Way of Incense, greatly influenced by the practice of Zen Buddhism. This 'art' is a path of learning, so complex that it takes a lifetime to become an incense master. It is said that to follow the way of *Kodo* is more demanding even than the fifteen years it takes to master the tea ceremony. During a *Kodo* incense ceremony, a delicate and precise preparation of special containers containing hot ash and different kinds of aloe wood are prepared. Aloe woods

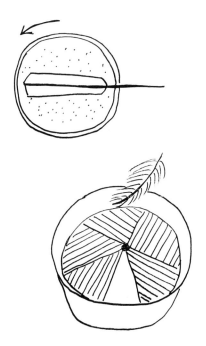

Hot ash in a Kodo pot, flattened with a stick (above) and a smudge bowl with a feather for spreading smoke

and agar woods from different parts of Indonesia and Indochina are used. Participants in the *Kodo* ceremony pass around the containers of incense and comment on the qualities of the aromas. One of the most important *Kodo* concepts is 'listening' to the aromas, which implies a deep and sensitive level of understanding and appreciation. *Kodo* is still very popular in Japan today; incense shops offer different blends to purchase and special groups study the aromas in order to develop and spiritually open the mind. *Kodo* ranks alongside the other classical Arts of Japan—*Sado* (The Way of Tea), *Kado* (The Way of Flowers) or *Budo* (The Martial Way). The Way of Incense is seen as a deeply spiritual path, where the incense fragrances used are a journey which leads to profound personal development.

This aromatic exploration across the world has taken in many aspects of culture, history and spiritual belief. At the end of it, I hope you marvel as I do at the rich heritage of incense use which is so widespread, even to this day. It is useful at this stage to summarize some of the key elements which recur time and time again across all traditions.

Incense is Protective

The use of aromatic plant ingredients means that their aromas, which are made up of special chemicals, spread into the air. These ingredients have been used for hundreds of years to cleanse the atmosphere and keep infection at bay, like the use of rosemary and juniper by ancient Greek physicians. From this practice, the idea that incense protects you and your space from negativity in any form may have developed, as we saw with the smudging practices of Native Americans.

Incense is a means of Spiritual Communication

From ancient Egyptian times, the idea that the smoke of incense travels from the physical to the unseen world—from matter to spirit and back—is echoed in many other traditions. Remember the Jewish tradition mentioned earlier and found in the old Testament, where God tells Moses that burning the incense will enable them to communicate. In Buddhist tradition too, the Buddha can be 'called' by burning fragrant aromas, and in Catholic churches incense enhances the appreciation of the 'presence of God.'

Incense is a tool for Spiritual Growth

The Japanese *Kodo* tradition is perhaps the most refined of all the spiritual paths of incense, with its intricate and deep appreciation of aromas. However, the Native Americans also revere their sacred herbs as means of transformation, renewal and spiritual opening, and across all traditions the practice of offering incense daily is a means of bringing an awareness of the subtle realms into everyday life.

Incense is Purifying

The aromas of certain incense ingredients like frankincense, copal, white sage or borneo camphor have very penetrating, pungent aromas which are cleansing to the lungs, deepening the breathing and cleansing the respiratory passages. All incense traditions link the use of incense to the breath, to improving the supply of air, oxygen and also life-force—called *prana* in India and *qi* in China. Doing this is seen as absolutely vital to life, vitality and spiritual awareness. In addition, the purifying effects of incense may help to boost the immune system.

Incense is Healing

In the Ayurvedic tradition of India, incense is used alongside physical application of aromatics to restore the balance between body, mind and spirit. The *curanderas* of Peru also use it to enhance their understanding of how to treat a patient. In many traditions, both historical and current, a dividing line between what is 'spiritual' and what is 'healing' does not exist. Both are aspects of one energy, the energy of Creation, which permeates all things and brings renewal. Incense helps to dissolve anxiety and brings a sense of peace.

Underlying all of these is a simple word—reverence. What does this mean? It can be a simple thanks, an awareness and gratitude for the abundance of Creation; it can also mean an acceptance that there is more to life, the Universe and everything than we can see with our eyes. There is room in our technological age for mystery, for that which cannot be explained but which can be felt. Across time, across continents, many of our fellow human beings have continued to express their reverence for this unseen energy which underlies all things, calling it different names, but being aware of its power. Incense—the way of smoke—opens the door to that understanding.

CHAPTER 3
INCENSE MATERIALS

IN THIS chapter, we shall discover twenty-five individual incense materials, each of which is easy to obtain and use in making your own incense blends—which we shall be doing in Chapter 4. Each one has a profile telling you its botanical name as well as its English name—this is important because when you buy materials, sometimes one English name covers several types of plant! You may also find that some of the ingredients we will be looking at are already in your kitchen cupboard—spices, for example—or even growing in your garden as herbs and flowers.

I have grouped the ingredients by plant parts—roots, woods/bark, leaves, resins/gums, fruits/seeds and flowers—for easy reference. You will find out how to prepare and store ingredients for use in making incense, discover the individual properties of these plants and learn some simple ways to combine them in incense combinations. I tend to use three or four ingredients in a blend, and when I list them,

the amount you would use would be a 'pinch' of each—that is, as much as you can pick up between your thumb and fingers in one go.

Roots

GINGER (*Zingiber officinale*). This aromatic fleshy root from China and India is becoming more and more popular in cooking, especially in Indian, Thai and Chinese recipes. There is quite a different aroma when you compare fresh root ginger to dried ginger powder. The fresh root has a fiery and zesty scent, sharp and penetrating; the dried root powder is much sweeter with a warm spiciness. For incense-blending purposes, ginger is best used in powder form. It contributes a gentle sweetness to blends, especially when combined with dried fruit peel like orange. The aroma of ginger is beneficial to the digestion; it stimulates the stomach, sometimes making the tummy rumble! It is good to use it if the appetite is sluggish or there is lack of interest in food. In Ayurvedic medicine, ginger is a very important warming remedy with a positive effect on the whole body; it is also a staple remedy in traditional Chinese medicine with positive effects on the respiratory and immune systems. Ginger also works well with other spices like cardamom or cinnamon to create pungent and pleasantly-scented incense—this type of combination would work well at Christmas time, because these aromas are often associated with warming winter cheer!

TURMERIC (*Curcuma domestica*). This bright yellow root is only available dry, either in pieces or ground up as a powder. It has a very subtle aroma, dry and earthy, slightly woody with a hint of sharpness. In cooking, it is used in Indian recipes to colour rice yellow, for example; like ginger, it has very beneficial effects on the digestion, but whereas ginger is heating, turmeric is more cooling and soothing both in its aromas and its effects. In Ayurvedic tradition turmeric is used as a cleansing and purifying remedy for the blood; you can also use it as a space-clearing incense ingredient. In terms of incense-making, one

important thing it will do is turn your blended mixture a bright golden yellow colour. In Indian tradition, yellow is very sacred—this is why monks often wear yellow or orange-yellow robes or wear garlands of golden yellow flowers. It is linked to the sun, the Source of Creation. If you want to make an incense with a strong visual link to the Creator, then combine some turmeric with frankincense, as well as other golden ingredients like sandalwood and lemon peel. Turmeric will add a soft earthy note to the aroma.

Woods and Barks

SANDALWOOD (*Santalum album*). This is one of the most famous of all incense ingredi-

Sandalwood Beads: fragrant gift from a Guru

ents. The fragrant wood is obtained from the trunks of trees growing particularly in the Mysore region of southern India. It is a light golden-brown wood with a rich soft and slightly spicy aroma at first, which becomes much deeper and woodier as it burns. This lovely wood is carved into statues, boxes and furniture, used in powder form as a cosmetic and as a cleansing ingredient in Ayurvedic medicine, distilled to produce an essential oil for perfumery and aromatherapy and used in the making of toiletries and soaps. Powder, sawdust and chippings of the precious wood are used for incense-making. Sandalwood production is a major industry in India, controlled by the government there, and in recent years illegal logging of trees has caused problems of supply.

Good herbalists or Indian spice merchants do sell sandalwood chippings or powder; the price has increased because of increasingly limited availability. However, if you want to make fine incense it is worth paying for. Sandalwood combined with frankincense and benzoin gum makes a wonderful base for any incense combination. It is also a key ingredient in Nag Champa incense sticks.

CEDARWOOD (*Cedrus atlantica, Cedrus deodar*). Here we have to be careful that we have the correct cedarwood, because thuja, our next wood, is also commonly called 'cedar'. True cedarwood trees are majestic giants often found in parks or botanical gardens; massive tent-like trees with branches trailing down to the ground and slightly prickly evergreen foliage. Now I am certainly not suggesting that you go and chop branches off these trees; however, any loose twigs or needles on the ground can be gathered, and more importantly the cones. These are often sticky with wonderfully aromatic drops of resin. They smell absolutely divine if burned outside over hot coals. Twigs or needles of cedar need to be chopped with secateurs into very small pieces for use in powdered incense combinations; they will still be in relatively large chunks compared with other ingredients so only small amounts are needed. Cedarwood combined with frankincense, pine and eucalyptus makes a wonderful fragrance combination for cleansing and purifying work.

Cedrus atlantica—the Atlas Cedar—is originally native to the Atlas mountains of North Africa; cedrus deodar is the Himalayan cedar. Using these ingredients in your own incense formulations brings you close to ancient sources of aromatic ingredients and the people who originally used them.

THUJA (*Thuja occidentalis*). This evergreen tree with soft aromatic foliage is also called Western or White Cedar and is native to the USA; it was introduced to Europe in the 16th century. The name thuja is actually derived from a Greek word meaning 'to fumigate';

the wood was burned to purify sickrooms in France. It is the type of cedar used in Native American smudge combinations as a cleansing and purifying aroma. A safety note: thuja foliage can irritate the skin, so if you are pruning a tree or collecting twigs and branches it is best to wear gloves and cover your arms to protect yourself.

Again, twigs or evergreen leaves can be cut up into very small pieces to use in powdered incense combinations, or twigs can be burned outside in a purifying aromatic fire. A wonderful incense combination to try would be thuja, juniper and European sage mixed together as a cleansing and strengthening blend of aromas. As all of these are powerful scents very little material is ever needed.

The aroma of burning thuja is very similar to that of Borneo Camphor which, as we have seen, is difficult to obtain in the West, so it acts as a reasonable alternative.

PINE (*Pinus sylvestris, Pinus nigra, Pinus maritima*)—Scots pine, black spruce and Corsican pine respectively. All these species of pine are very commonly found in woodland, parks and gardens all over the countryside; as well as having aromatic needles and twigs, they all produce sticky resin. Certain North American pine species also produce a very fine resin which smells somewhat like copal when burned. Pine was used by Native Americans to make highly aromatic fires to repel mosquitoes. A variety of pine called *Pinus succinifera* from the Baltic coast is actually the tree which produces resin which over millions of years turns into amber, often used in jewellery. The three species mentioned above vary slightly, with the Scots pine being sharp, black spruce sweeter and Corsican pine deeply pungent. For incense-making, gather needles and small twigs from under the tree, and again look for cones, which are very aromatic. Dried pine needles and twigs burn incredibly fast, so add them to glowing coals slowly to inhale their full effect. Pine needles work very well with eucalyptus leaves and frankincense grains to create a beautiful uplifting incense aroma with a finer energetic effect, very heady and clearing. Inhaling the aroma of pine clears the lungs and improves the breathing; it helps support the respiratory and immune systems.

CINNAMON (*Cinnamonum zeylanicum*). This is the true cinnamon, native to Sri Lanka and other parts of Indochina, often used today as cinna-

Cinnamon Bark

mon sticks or powdered bark in sweet and savoury cooking and drinks. As we have seen, cinnamon was and still is an important ingredient in Indian, Chinese and Japanese incense blends. In ancient times another variety, cassia (*Cinnamonum cassia*) was also popular. The inner bark of the cinnamon tree has been used for thousands of years in East Asia as a cooking spice, a digestive and cleansing remedy with beneficial effects on the kidneys the respiratory systems and once again as an ingredient in fragrant incense. Cinnamon is easy to buy and needs to be stored in an airtight jar in a cool dry place after opening because it tends to lose its aroma quickly when exposed to the air. For incense-making, the sticks are better; they can easily be pounded to smaller pieces using a pestle and mortar. Cinnamon combined with cardamom seeds and sandalwood is a won-

derful warming combination to burn, especially in the winter months when it is cold outside and life feels depressing! Try adding some orange peel to the blend for a fruity note.

Resins and Gums

FRANKINCENSE (*Boswellia carterii, Boswellia sacra*). We have already discussed this material extensively; it is possibly the most classic of all incense ingredients and has been so for thousands of years. The *carterii* species is from Somalia, and the sacra species from the Dhofar valley in Oman. In aromatherapy,

A Wooden Casket of Frankincense

Myrrh—a tree-gum, broken here into small crystalline pieces

essential oils distilled from resin from both species are used in massage; the Oman frankincense is preferred for its deeper richer aroma. The trees survive in very hostile desert conditions; to seal and repair any cracks in their bark they produce drops of very sticky aromatic resin which dries and hardens in the sun. Dark yellow or brown frankincense granules are considered inferior; pale yellow or whitish granules are the best quality. Frankincense grains can be obtained from good herbalists. They need to be ground to a powder using a pestle and mortar if you are combining them with other aromatic ingredients in an incense blend.

Frankincense with benzoin gum and myrrh makes a resin trio which creates a wonderfully exotic and 'ancient' aroma. Adding sandalwood to the mix gives a more Indian scent. These ingredients are excellent as a combination for purifying space before meditation or yoga practice. The aroma of pure frankincense burning is warm, deep and resiny with a hint of musk.

MYRRH (*Commiphora myrrha*). This shrub grows to thirty feet in height in geographical locations not unlike those of frankincense. It has very sharp thorns and produces a reddish orange gum which dries in the sun. Myrrh has a characteristic bittersweet aroma, and when it is ground to a powder it has a soft pink colour. The chemistry of myrrh makes it soluble in water, unlike frankincense; in the Middle East it has been used for centuries to cleanse and deodorize the mouth as well as protect the teeth. Myrrh's mysterious fragrance was regarded as an astonishing in ancient times, and revered in the Old Testament in the Song of Solomon. This is quite hard for us to understand in modern times when our perfume preferences are quite different. Yet it was used in embalming, in medicine to heal wounds, as a perfume and a cosmetic, as well as an incense ingredient. Along with frankincense and gold, it was given to Jesus at his birth; it was considered precious to the same degree as that metal. Myrrh in incense terms combines well with orange peel and cardamom seeds to create a very warming and interesting aroma, very supportive and fortifying in winter.

BENZOIN GUM (*Styrax benzoin*). This wonderful reddish-orange crystalline gum comes from the cracks and fissures in the bark of a tropical tree, native to Sumatra and Java. It has an astonishing sweet and vanilla-like odour which is characteristic of incense blends used in Bali, Thailand and Sumatra. It can be obtained from good herbal suppliers. In Eastern medicinal traditions, benzoin is used to help respiratory complaints; in the west benzoin is probably best known as an ingredient in 'Friar's Balsam', an old-fashioned remedy for coughs and colds. In Southern Europe in Roman times they called it 'silphion' and used it as a room fragrance and an expensive medicine. Again like other resins it needs to be ground to a powder using a pestle and mortar to mix with other incense ingredients. It has a very long-lasting aroma, prolonging the effects of any blend made with it; in perfumery, benzoin is known as a 'fixative'. Its

Pieces of
Benzoin gum

fine fragrance can be appreciated on its own; it releases a sweet vanilla-like aroma with a hint of cinnamon. If you want to blend it, I suggest trying benzoin with cinnamon and sandalwood for a woody, yet soft, sweet, aroma that is very tranquil and uplifting.

ROSEMARY (*Rosmarinus officinalis*). This tough but beautiful aromatic shrub is native to the Mediterreanean, but grows successfully in more northern climates too. The hotter and drier the environment, the more powerful and pungent it smells. Rosemary is well-known

A Rosemary pot is easily found
in a supermarket

as a cooking and medicinal herb; it was also used by the ancient Greeks as an incense, thrown onto the fire to crackle and releasing a wonderful penetrating aromatic smoke. If you grow it in your garden you can cut branches of it, tie them into bundles and hang them upside-down in a shed to dry. Then they can be burned outside in dramatic and beautiful cleansing ceremonies where the fragrant smoke curls up to the sky. For use indoors, smaller branches of rosemary can be dried in a warm cupboard until the leaves fall off the stems. Keep the dried leaves in an airtight jar; when you want to use them they can be pounded, using a pestle and mortar. For an incense combination, try rosemary with eucalyptus leaves and lavender flowers: a soft and beautifully fresh combination. It has a very powerful aroma, so is best burnt in the daytime or early evening—else it can keep you awake!

MARJORAM (*Origanum marjorana*). This small and delicately-fragranced herb is another from the Mediterranean. It grows close to the ground and produces small, aromatic dark-green leaves, and clusters of tiny purple flowers at the height of summer. It is good to pick for drying just before it flowers, because then there are the maximum numbers of leaves available. Drying takes the water content out of the plant tissue, leaving the essential oils and other aromatic ingredients behind, so when the leaves are burned they give off the maximum aroma. Marjoram is easy to grow yourself in the garden and also works well in pots. Although it is a perennial, it can be damaged by frost, so it needs protection in the winter. The ancient Egyptians grew marjoram and used it medicinally, and it was also popular in Greek and Roman times as a culinary herb and soothing remedy. Marjoram has

a calming effect on the nervous system and makes a wonderful blend combined with lavender flowers and peppermint leaves. The scent of the mixture is soft, sweet and slightly fresh. It is good to use for sensitive emotional states, when spirits are low and there is a need for gentle comfort.

PEPPERMINT (*Mentha x piperita*). This popular herb is a hybrid, a cross between Spearmint and Water Mint. It is incredibly tough and can be invasive if you plant it in your garden; try growing it in a large pot. Peppermint is the most pungent of all the mints, it makes a wonderful aromatic tea. Again, if you want to dry leaves for incense-making then choose them before the plant flowers; tie small bunches of stalks together and hang them upside-down in an airing cupboard. When the leaves come away from the stalks easily, then store them in an airtight jar. Peppermint leaves were hugely popular with the Romans, who invented mint sauce as an accompaniment to meats; they liked to decorate their tables with peppermint and wear garlands of it to banquets. A lovely fresh incense combination would be peppermint, eucalyptus and myrtle leaves; this would have an uplifting effect, very useful for cleansing a space of any negative energies, or soothing and calming the breathing before meditation. Peppermint is refreshing to the mind, unlike rosemary, which is stimulating; so this combination can be burned in the evenings.

MYRTLE (*Myrtus communis*). This shrub too is a native of the Mediterranean. It has lovely reddish stalks and dark green shiny aromatic leaves which smell like a combination of bergamot and eucalyptus. In the summer, myrtle produces exquisite white and

gold flowers which were traditionally used in the south of Europe as a facial wash. Myrtle likes a warm climate but will grow in more northerly latitudes, especially against a south-facing wall for shelter. In ancient Greek times, Myrtle was considered sacred to the feminine energy symbolized by Artemis, or Diana as she was known to the Romans. Branches of myrtle were burned in sacred groves; and for many hundreds of years in Europe, myrtle sprigs were essential in a bride's bouquet. Myrtle branches can be cut and hung up in a shed to dry; tie

a paper bag around the bundle to collect the leaves as they drop off the stalks. These make wonderful aromatic kindling for a fire outside, and the leaves can be stored in an airtight jar for incense blending or tea-making—the infusion is delicious. Blend myrtle with frankincense and rose petals for a glorious incense to invoke the sacred feminine.

EUCALYPTUS (*Eucalyptus globulus* and many other species). Eucalyptus trees are native to Australia, though they have been introduced successfully to many other countries like Spain and the USA, and also to northern latitudes. They are very tough and yet graceful trees with highly aromatic wood and leaves. The leaves tend to fall regularly, so they are easy to collect for incense-making; the important thing is that they must be completely dry before you store them, so lay them on sheets of absorbent paper to make sure. Then break the leaves into the smallest pieces possible before adding them to incense blends.

The aborigines of Australia make fires of eucalyptus leaves and wood to help with respiratory infections, as well as to keep away mosquitoes. Burning eucalyptus leaves outside in the summer can help to keep invading insects at bay. Eucalyptus works wonderfully with other herbs like rosemary and sage to create very pungent and cleansing combinations, excellent for smudging healing spaces after clients have left. Native American healers will not work in a space unless it has been properly smudged first, and once the treatment is over they cleanse it again. This is an excellent practice to adopt.

SAGE (*Salvia officinalis*). This is the European sage, which is much milder in its effect than desert and white sage, the US species mentioned earlier in the book. Deciding what kind of sage to use is a matter of personal choice; if you want the very powerful effects of Native American sage for smudging, then it is best to purchase smudge sticks from herbal suppliers. Garden sage, the European cooking herb, can also be used for a very beautiful cleansing aroma, which is softer, sweeter and gentler. It depends on whether it is important to you to use herbs that are native to where you live; we will return

to this idea in Chapter 4. If you want to dry garden sage, cut long stalks and bind them into bunches, to hang upside down in a warm cupboard. The stalks and leaves can then be cut up and ground into incense combinations. Sage is wonderful combined with juniper berries and rosemary to create a more European style cleansing combination with a herbal and pungent aroma; it also works very well with frankincense and lemon peel for a lighter and more resiny effect. Sage is one of the most important incense herbs for space clearing, which means cleansing the atmosphere of negativity.

Fruits and Seeds

CARDAMOM (*Elettaria cardamomum*). The best quality cardamom pods are sold in specialist Indian grocers; there are two types. Green

pods are the sweetest, and there are also black pods that smell smokier. For incense-making purposes I prefer the green pods. They need to be split open, and the tiny black aromatic seeds can then be pounded into the incense blend. The ancient Egyptians, Greeks and Romans all used cardamom medicinally, showing how plants travelled vast distances even in those times—cardamom is native to India and grows all over the Far East. It is a cousin of ginger, and the two plants look very similar. It is a vital ingredient in Ayurvedic medicine for treating lung and other respiratory complaints as well as for supporting the immune system; in Indian cooking, cardamom pods are boiled in milk to make a fortifying drink and are used extensively in savoury and sweet recipes. Cardamom itself has a fascinating aroma—powerful, sweet and spicy. For an incense combination try it with sandalwood and orange peel for a sweet, woody and tranquil aroma, with a hint of fruit and spice. It has a very warming and cheering effect on the spirits, particularly in the cold winter months.

CORIANDER SEED (*Coriandrum sativum*). Coriander is a herb with lovely aromatic green leaves which are often used as a garnish in Indian and Eastern recipes. The plant produces tiny aromatic seeds which have a sweet and gently spicy aroma. It is native to southern Europe and western Asia, and is used across the whole of that vast region. Coriander seeds have been found in the tombs of ancient Egyptian pharaohs such as Tutankhamun as part of the extensive collection of herbs, spices and resins left there to support the king in the afterlife. The Egyptians used the seeds to flavour meat dishes, and possibly for medicinal purposes. The seeds are also used in traditional Chinese medicine for nausea and digestive upsets.

Although coriander is easy to grow as a herb, if you want supplies of the seeds it is best to go to a good herbalist. Coriander seeds need to be pounded to a powder in a pestle and mortar for incense combinations; they work well with ginger powder, benzoin gum and lemon peel for a sweet, mildly spicy and vanilla-like aroma with a hint of citrus. This is a very pleasant incense to create a relaxing atmosphere.

BLACK PEPPER (*Piper nigrum*). The aromatic sun-dried fruits of the black pepper vine produce one of the most well-known spices on the planet. Native to India and now produced extensively in Malaysia, Indonesia, Madagascar and China, it is one of the most traded spices in the world. Black pepper is an amazingly vigorous climbing vine with heart-shaped leaves, and clusters of flowers which turn into the fruit—peppercorns.

In Indian Ayurvedic and traditional Chinese practice, the use of black pepper as a medicine goes back at least 4000 years; it is generally used to help the digestive system and to warm the body when there is immune dysfunction. Black pepper is seen in both traditions as strengthening, both physically and emotionally—'to help you take heart' and keep on keeping on! The idea of using black pepper in incense might make you think of sneezing, but when it is combined with other spices and ingredients it adds a warm and pungent note to blends. Simply add a few twists from the pepper mill to a combination of benzoin gum, sandalwood and cinnamon for a lovely rich spicy combination, a wonderful help to the breathing in winter months.

JUNIPER BERRIES (*Juniperus communis*). Juniper is a tough, evergreen, prickly shrub with sharp needles and it is native to Scandinavia, Siberia and northern Europe. It produces large berries that take two years to turn black, which is when they are most aromatic. Apart from flavouring gin, juniper is also used in many traditional German and Scandinavian recipes, and in Switzerland a jam made with juniper berries is eaten to help boost the immune system. In the western herbal tradition, juniper is seen as very cleansing, particularly to the kidneys and lymphatic system. It was used as far afield as ancient Egypt in antiquity; records show it was an ingredient in the embalming process, and branches of the evergreen shrub and berries were burned to cleanse the air. The aroma of crushed ripe berries is sharp, green and fresh with woody notes. For an incense blend they need to be ground in a pestle and mortar before being mixed with other ingredients. For a really cleansing formula, try juniper with European sage and cedarwood leaves. The aroma of the blend would be deep, woody and smoky with strong, fresh and pungent notes. This would be a very good blend to use for outdoor space-cleansing ceremonies.

LEMON (*Citrus limonum*). The lemon tree is one of the large family of citrus trees, originally from China, and since successfully introduced all over the globe.

It is evergreen with beautiful lance-shaped shiny green leaves; it produces creamy white flowers and then large yellow lemon  fruit. Some of the best lemons come from Sicily in the southern Mediterranean, but fine ones are also produced in Spain, Israel and the USA. The peel of the fruit is what we need for incense purposes; it contains sacs of essential oil, which is why it is so aromatic. To prepare it, wash the lemon in hot water and then use a very sharp knife or a lemon zester to pare away strips of peel. Try to avoid the white pith underneath, which is bitter. Place the strips of peel in a clean dish and let them dry out in a warm cupboard; then store them in a clean glass jar. Lemon peel adds a sharp tangy citrus note to any incense blend; a favourite combination of mine is sandalwood, lemon peel and frankincense. This creates a beautiful subtle aroma, woody, resiny and light, which is excellent to create a relaxed and fragrant atmosphere.

SWEET ORANGE (*Citrus sinensis*). The orange is another evergreen citrus tree, closely related to mandarin and bergamot. The sweet orange is the fruit you normally buy to eat; there is a bitter orange with a wrinkled skin which is used for making marmalade. Sweet oranges are grown all over the world, especially in Florida, Israel and Spain. As with all citrus fruit, they originated in China and the Far East, and were brought to Europe by Arab traders in the early centuries of the last millennium. They were a luxury food for hundreds of years, only available to the wealthy.

As with lemon, the peel is used in incense-making. It is important to wash it before preparing it to peel, because any waxes which have been used during transportation need to be removed. Dry the peel as described for lemons. Orange has a much sweeter aroma than lemon, soft and piercing, and blends with many different aromas. One combination to try is orange peel with peppermint leaves and lavender flowers—this smells like summer, all the aromas of fruit herbs and flowers combined.

Flowers

LAVENDER (*Lavandula angustifolia*). This is a beautiful aromatic bush which features in many people's gardens. There are many species of lavender with purple, lilac, pink, white or dark blue flowers. All can be used for incense purposes; the white flowers are particularly pungent compared with the sweeter purple and pink ones. It is fun to experiment. Lavender was brought to the UK in Roman times—its name comes from the Latin *lavare* (to wash). It has a tradition of being used to cleanse and deodorize the skin, as well as to keep moths away from clothes!

Cut your lavender for incense-making just as the flowers are at their best. Tie bunches of stalks together and hang them upside-down in an airing cupboard, with a paper bag around each one to catch any falling flowers. Once the stalks are dry, shake all the flowers into the bag and pour them into a clean jar. The stalks make good kindling for a fire outdoors. Lavender flowers give off a soft and headily sweet aroma in an incense combination Try them with marjoram and lemon peel for a soft and relaxing fragrance; they work in a similar way with sandalwood and orange peel.

ROSE (*Rosa* species). The rose is the source of one of the most ideal yet elusive fragrances—there are so many varieties, all hybridized originally from parents like the damask rose (*Rosa damascena*) or the cabbage rose (*Rosa centifolia*). Modern gardeners are becoming interested once more in growing scented flowers, so 'old-fashioned' roses are back in vogue. If you have a fine fragrant rose nearby which you like, then it is perfect to dry some petals for incense purposes. Some rose aromas are sweet, some more citrus-like and some very musky, for example, so it is a question of personal taste; find one that appeals to you. Carefully pick some perfect blooms before they are fully open. Separate off the petals individually and lay them on kitchen paper on a baking tray, and put them in the bottom of the oven on the coolest possible temperature overnight, leaving the oven door open slightly. Then store them in a clean jar. Rose combines ideally with frankincense and sandalwood for an Indian-type aromatic incense, beautifully floral and woody. To the Indian sages rose was a perfect aroma in itself, sacred to the gods, a symbol of spiritual attunement and sanctity; to many cultures, the rose is the symbol of divine love.

JASMINE (*Jasminum officinale*). Tiny white jasmine flowers are incredibly fragrant; in India they are used to decorate the statues of gods and goddesses. There are different jasmine species; in India, *Jasminum grandiflorum* is popular because it has larger blooms. There is also a winter yellow jasmine that grows well in more northerly climates. Many people now have jasmine growing in their gardens; its aroma is particularly fine at dusk, when the night-flying moths are looking for nectar. It is possible to pick jasmine flowers for drying, but you have to handle them very carefully. It is best to lay them on sheets of absorbent paper and place them in an airing cupboard to dry them out then store them in an airtight jar. Jasmine is heady, musky and sweet in incense; it is used to make many formulations in India. Try it with sandalwood and benzoin gum for a beautiful woody and yet soft aroma, very tranquil and soothing. Only a tiny amount is ever needed because the aroma is powerful; it helps to ground and calm you when you are stressed and anxious. I also enjoy it with orange peel and myrrh for an intriguing aroma with floral and citrus hints, and a bitter sweetness.

As we have seen, collecting and storing incense ingredients can be quite a task. Many are available as dried supplies from good herbalists. It is pleasant and interesting, though, to harvest plants in your

Keep your jars clearly labelled

own garden and prepare them for incense use. It is a way of experiencing the scents of your garden when the seasons change and it allows you to blend them in ways that are creative to you. When you have collected and dried ingredients they can stay potent for over a year; if there is any sign of mould or decay they must be discarded. This is why careful drying is so important. Keep your jars clearly labelled with the plant variety so you know what is what, and also write the date when you stored the ingredient. Clean glass jam jars are ideal containers. If you really start making incense in earnest you might need an extra kitchen cupboard....

CHAPTER 4
HOW TO BURN INCENSE

IN THIS chapter, we shall look at how actually to burn incense, and the best way to do so safely and effectively. These guidelines should be studied and followed carefully, even if you have experimented with incense before. The aim is to enhance and improve your personal space, not to necessitate a visit from the fire brigade! It is important to be sensible and prepare your space carefully, whether you are working inside or outside. Fire is something that has to be treated with respect.

The Fire Element

Fire is one of the elemental forces of nature. Western tradition places it with three other elements of air, earth and water; eastern traditions add a fifth, called by various names including 'ether'. In Indian Ayurvedic tradition the element of fire is the transforming power of the Universe, initiating change, moving other elements from one state to another: for example, water to steam to air. It is a dynamic and creative force echoing the power of the Sun, the creative Cosmic Source. Many Hindu gods are shown surrounded by fire, indicating their transformative powers. Fire is an element that changes the state of matter (for example the physical pieces of plant material in an incense blend) into a more subtle representation—smoke—which can then travel to different levels of cosmic consciousness, transforming human awareness as it does so.

While fire can be transforming, like any element if it gets out of control it can do damage. Fire in the body is fever, which if left unchecked can threaten life. In our very controlled living environment we are often not used to handling the pure elemental forces in the way that our ancestors did every day. Not long ago, every British home relied on a fire which was kindled every day, kept burning to provide heat for cooking and warming dwellings, and banked down at night to keep coals hot for the next day to start again. Nowadays we are not so used to such practices, though they continue in many other parts of the world. If we are going to use the element of fire, it must be done with safety and care.

Safety Inside and Outside

If you are going to use incense inside your home, first you need to think about where to burn it. It needs to be kept safely away from straying curtains that might blow across from an open window, for example. It also needs to be away from any expensive items of furniture, for example wooden tables, or soft furnishings like lampshades or cushions—just in case a tiny burning ember flies into the air. When incense burns, it does generate smoke, so it is best kept away from pale painted walls to avoid stains.

Stick incense holders are very common and are made in a whole variety of different shapes and sizes. They are designed to catch the falling ash as the incense burns. I always place the holder on a base which I have made out of a twelve-inch diameter circle of cardboard completely covered in aluminium foil. I use this base for all indoor incense-burning equipment, and place it in the middle of a small table well away from other furniture.

The way to burn the kinds of incense blends we shall be making is to use a charcoal pellet in a ceramic incense pot, more like the Japanese use. These are made to withstand the heat generated by the charcoal. If you want to buy a pot for incense burning, it is best to go to a Japanese or Indian shop to get the right kind of ceramic container; alternatively you need to look for a small glazed pot which is quite thick walled to withstand the temperature. Incense can be burned in metal dishes, but again you would need a protective base underneath to safeguard furniture.

Charcoal pellets are another key piece of equipment, and these can be bought from incense suppliers or from hardware stores. You need a pair of tongs to hold pellets as you light them; they are specially coated to ignite straight away with a kind of crackling noise. It's best to do this outside. Hold the pellet up with the tongs as it catches fire, wait until it is lightly glowing and then place it in the ceramic container. You can then bring it inside to use with your incense.

When you make an incense blend, you grind the ingredients to a powder, as we have already seen. This is best done using a pestle and mortar; they can be bought from good cookware shops. The best ones are made of marble. Buy one especially to use for incense-making. Place your ingredients in the bottom of the container (a much smaller amount than in the illustration!) and use the pestle to grind them with small circular motions, until they form a loose powder made of smaller pieces of the ingredients. Then pour the blend into a small saucer or dish and it is ready to use.

Pick up a pinch of the blend between your fingers, and slowly sprinkle it onto the hot charcoal pellet. Then sit quietly and inhale the aroma of the scented smoke. It is best to use only a little at a time, because instantly you will realize that the aromas are

Marble pestle and mortar with frankincense awaiting pulverisation

powerful. You may feel initially that you only want to sprinkle the blend on once, until you get used to the fragrance; or you may want to add more blend after a few moments. It is up to you. In Japan, in the *Kodo* ceremony, the fragrance is allowed to permeate the air for some while before more is added. Once a charcoal pellet is lit, it will continue glowing until it is pale grey and has become ash. You can leave it until it is cool to dispose of it outside (you can dig it into your garden, for plants like ash) or you can pour a little water onto it to put it out. Then wipe out your pot with a piece of kitchen towel and it is ready to use again.

If you are using a Native American smudge stick, then this should be lit outside, applying a match to the end of the bundle. Wait for it to ignite, then blow the flame out, so the bundle is smoking, and put it back in your incense pot, smoking end downwards. Wave your feather over the pot, and that will be enough to keep the bundle glowing and producing smoke while you smudge a person or a space by carrying the pot around a room. Be careful not to waft the feather too vigorously or you could send tiny red-hot embers into the air, and that is a fire risk.

Another way to experience sacred smoke is outside. This is a practice which is very common across the world but less so in Western Europe. It means making a special fire in which you will burn selected aromatic woods and leaves. Obviously, deciding to make an aromatic fire outside depends on certain factors like where you live; if you have a town garden, then you are in your own private space, but you would be advised to keep a fire small so as not to annoy your neighbours! If you have a wider area around you, it is not such a problem; you could even create a special place for sacred fire. In California, many houses have special pits lined with stones built into their gardens for the purpose of enjoying fires outdoors. Indeed, it is truly atmospheric and wonderful to sit around a glowing fire under a night sky, especially if that fire is also aromatic.

One way to keep an outdoor fire small is to use a little outdoor portable barbecue (minus the meat!). To keep yourself and the area of your fire safe, don't make your fire too close to your house or to wooden sheds or fences. Set your small barbecue container on the ground, preferably on a paving or concrete base. Just place a layer of aromatic kindling like dried lavender stalks, rosemary or myrtle branches in the bottom of the container and cover that with small pieces of charcoal. The kindling should catch fire quickly because it is dry, and you can add more branches to keep the flames going until the charcoal glows. Dried kindling burns quickly without making too much smoke. Once your bed of charcoal is hot, you can then sprinkle an incense blend over it as described previously. When you want to put out the fire slowly pour water over the charcoal and leave it to cool.

It is interesting to explore how different it is to experience incense in the open air. To me, there is a sense of space, of connection with the heavens that you can see by simply looking at the sky, and with nature by looking around you. Being outside with incense encourages a kind of expansion that is partly due to the slowing of the breath but also to the extension of your senses taking in all that surrounds you.

Using incense indoors is quite different; I feel it immediately brings a more meditative quality to the space. It settles the mind and the senses and encourages a different kind of contemplation, a more inner attention to oneself. It can completely change your mood and feelings, especially if you have been stressed or anxious. It brings a sense of clarity and calm, clearing away negativity.

It is good to explore these different aspects for yourself and decide what you think their qualities are. Incense—the way of smoke—is a personal journey, and it is yours to experience. By bringing aromatic ingredients into your environment, you are starting to relate to your space in a way which may be new to you, but is in fact very ancient, as old as the first camp fires on the open plains our distant ancestors wandered millennia ago, before civilization began. It brings a sense of connection across time, a sense of the rhythms of life, of the difference between night and day, inside and outside, energy and matter, spirit and human—and awareness that this is all part of a whole, the Oneness expressed by the Chinese as the Tao; the web of life, of existence itself.

CHAPTER 5
SCENT AND CEREMONY

THIS CHAPTER is all about how to use incense in your daily life. It answers questions like 'how often', 'what for', and 'why?'. First it is helpful to remind ourselves of some of the traditional uses of incense which we have already seen. Remember, all over the world incense is still used as an offering of thanks or to clear and cleanse a space, to mark a special event or to welcome in a new phase of life. These kinds of uses can be easily incorporated into your experience of daily living.

Why? Why should it be important to do these things? Well, perhaps because incense is a sign of something special, and maybe our lives need markers, moments that create memories, moments of connection. Perhaps in the drone of the machine we have lost touch with the rhythms of the earth, sun, moon and sky. If we think of special occasions, perhaps Christmas springs to mind, but for many people that feast is a food-filled excuse to concentrate on buying things, far removed from the spirit of what Christmas really

means. Creating moments of ceremony for yourself and your family and friends is a way of sharing sacred time and space in simple joy; and by our repeating such cycles, gradually they take on a life of their own, they become part of the fabric of existence. This is so for many people around the world today who still use incense for their personal expression of something special, something sacred, something beyond the 'seen'. Even if these words cannot communicate this sense to you, perhaps you can 'feel' what I mean. Remember—in the *Kodo* ceremony, they 'listen' to the aromas. Creating simple rituals with incense can help to bring a deeper meaning to everyday existence.

The first way to experience a simple ceremony is to light a small tea-light candle and, from it, a stick of incense; and use it either to start your day or to help you finish it. Each of these times is slightly different. In the morning, lighting a candle greets the new day, and a small stick of incense refreshes the air as you take a few moments of quiet to pause before

and dash out of the house. However, if you get up a little earlier and try this routine, you may be surprised at how much more centred you end up feeling as you leave. If you decide to light your candle and incense at the end of the day, it reflects an energy of winding down, of rest, of the night drawing in. As you pause and breathe in the aroma, concentrate on that and not on the many thoughts chasing around your head. Then notice how you feel inside. Differently, I would imagine; calmer, I hope.

We are now going to explore some more occasions where the use of an incense blend could help to enhance the atmosphere and add a sense of the sacred. These are important life-events when you may like to try creating a special ceremony. I will give ideas for ways to prepare the space as well as incense blends to make, but of course you can experiment and do whatever feels right to you. Follow your intuition and choose for yourself. The 'way of smoke' is your own journey.

Moving Home

Moving is one of the most stressful events which can take place in life, and perhaps among all the 'busyness' of organizing it the idea of incorporating an

getting into your routine. This could sound improbable if your current routine is to get up, get dressed, incense ceremony might seem like one thing too many. Yet in many cultures, moving would not be contemplated without it. Why? Because the burning of incense helps to cleanse the space of your energy which has occupied it for a time, so as to prepare it for the person coming along next. Some space-clearing teachers suggest that incense also helps to cleanse the energy if you are finding it hard to sell or rent your property—because your energy is too tied to it, and therefore nothing new can come in.

To prepare for the ceremony, in a pestle and mortar put a pinch each of frankincense grains, European sage leaves and eucalyptus leaves and grind these to a powder. Then go around your space and clap your hands loudly in all the rooms and especially in all the corners. This activates and livens up the energy inside. Clean the space thoroughly (I mean physically, with some 'elbow-grease'), and on a table place a clean cloth, with some fresh flowers and a crystal, if you like. Light a candle. Then light a charcoal pellet outside and place it in your incense pot, bring it in and set it on the table with the other items. Add a pinch of your blend and sit quietly for a few moments, inhaling the aroma. Now express a few thoughts. For example, it is important to thank the space for what it has given you, to appreciate

what you have enjoyed about being there and to express your good wishes to those who come next, as you move on. These are the kinds of affirmations you may like to make, and it is good to express them out loud. Then you may like to listen to a piece of music which inspires you, as you continue to smell the wonderful aroma; let your creative imagination take you forward into thoughts of a new beginning.

You can also adapt this routine for moving into a new space; in fact, once again, many cultures would regard this as essential. Create a small altar with candles and flowers; carry your incense pot around the empty space before you move in, or use a smudge stick to spread sacred smoke through and cleanse; accompany this with clapping, singing, drums or bells to make the space ready to receive you. Affirm thanks to those who have left it, and your positive intentions for life in this new environment. Then you are ready to move in!

Celebrating Christmas

Certain aromas are crucial to the 'smell of Christmas'—things like cinnamon and orange. These warm, spicy fragrances are very cheering in the middle of winter and contribute to a special sense of anticipation; they are of course used in many Christmas recipes as well. Another wonderful aroma is pine, because the scent of an evergreen tree brought into the house is an essential part of Christmas preparations. You can combine pinches of dried pine needles, small pieces of cinnamon bark and dried orange peel together and use this as a wonderful Christmas incense. It has a deliciously uplifting aroma. A good time to burn this is late on Christmas Eve, as you wait for the coming of Christmas Day. The incense helps to create a wonderful atmosphere. You can also add some frankincense or myrrh granules to the blend; children will be fascinated if you tell them these are the actual gifts that the Wise Men brought to Jesus. It brings the words of the Bible so actively to life and gives real meaning to the story.

Celebrating a Wedding

In many cultures, incense is crucial to wedding celebrations; for example, we have seen how in Arab countries the wedding clothes are hung over precious burning aromatic ingredients to sanctify them for three days beforehand. This particular practice may not be to western tastes, yet there are some lovely ways in which you could prepare and enhance the space for a wedding. These days it is becoming more common for ceremonies to take place in a whole variety of locations, not just in places of worship. Many people choose to get married outdoors, for example. Here is a chance to think about aromas that work either inside or outside. For example, to work inside, choose a subtle combination of aromas such as a pinch each of rose petals, sandalwood and orange peel. For an outside gathering, something more pungent like a pinch each of frankincense, rosemary and myrtle would give a wonderful scent of burning aromatic wood. Make sure to burn only a small amount at a time so as not to make too much smoke in one go. It is lovely to have the scent in the space when people arrive for the ceremony; it helps to create a really special atmosphere.

Creating a Sacred Space for Yoga or Meditation

Burning incense is crucial if you want to prepare a space for either of these spiritual practices. In India it is vital because of the symbolic nature of incense ingredients, their purifying properties and also the involvement of the element of fire, transforming the physical particles of plant material into a more subtle

of sandalwood, frankincense and cardamom, to strengthen the energy of the heart and the breath, both of which are fundamental to good practice. Remember to pound the ingredients together well before sprinkling them onto the charcoal—this improves the all-round aroma.

Celebrating the seasons

The Celts, one of the ancient pre-Christian peoples of the British Isles, revered the points in the year when the seasons changed. They had a very different kind of calendar from ours today, one which was closely linked to their experience of growing crops and taking care of cattle. They started their new Year at what we now call All Saints Day (1st November) which they called *Samhain*; this was when they sowed winter wheat, which they hoped would grow swiftly in the early spring. Then, in the depths of winter, around the winter solstice on December 21st—which was calculated with astonishing accuracy by their temples and barrows (such as New Grange in Ireland)—they had a midwinter fire festival. They burned huge logs (the origin of the Yule log) to make the biggest fire they could, in order to make sure the sun would return. They would also

form—smoke—as a means of building a bridge to spirit. Whether you practise yoga or meditation alone or in a class situation, preparation of the space using incense enhances the mental focus that is necessary to still the chattering mind before contemplation.

Classic incense blend sticks like Nag Champa create an instantly beautiful atmosphere, or you can make a wonderful warming blend of a pinch each eat stores of carefully-hoarded food (the origin of the Christmas feast) as a statement of faith that the coming year would feed them once more. By the first of February, when the first green shoots appeared through the snow, they would celebrate *Imbolc*, the feast of the ewes, and on the first of May a fire festival, *Beltain*, when cattle were run through fires to cleanse them, and young couples jumped over the embers to show they were married. Finally, on the first of August, they celebrated the fruits of the harvest and the bounty of their cattle at *Lughnasadh*, the festival of Lugh the god of sun and light.

This cycle shows how ancient peoples lived in harmony with the seasons, accepting light and dark, sun and moon, life, death and rebirth as part of the harmony of all things. It is an unfortunate fact of modern life that such awareness tends to pass us by. However, if you are a gardener, you cannot help but notice the seasons turning; if you like to walk outside in nature you will observe it happening too. Change is the nature of life.

I like to mark the four sacred dates of the Celtic calendar—*Samhain, Imbolc, Beltain* and *Lughnasadh*—each time by making a small fire outside at night. If it rains around the date, I do it as close as I can to the time. I burn mostly European sage, rosemary and myrtle, as this cleansing combination smells so good on the night air. I stand under the stars and in the quiet of the night I feel the earth under my feet, and my connection to the sky above my head. I smell the sacred smoke as well as the different seasonal aromas—flowers in the summer, damp earth in the autumn—as well as feeling the difference in the temperatures of the changing seasons. I am conscious of the earth turning, the seasons turning, and my life turning too, in the never-ending circle of the cosmic dance.

The Moon Cycle

The moon also follows its rhythm, from new to waxing to full to waning to dark. It gives its name to the menstrual cycle in women: thirteen lunar rather than twelve solar cycles in a year. Studies have shown that regular observation of the moon affects the pituitary gland in the brain. The pituitary controls hormones, particularly in women; this can bring the menstrual cycle into rhythm with the moon so that ovulation happens when it is full and menstruation when it is dark. Ancient feminine rituals that celebrated lunar energy worked very much in tandem with lunar changes, venerating the divine Feminine as a goddess carrying the horned moon on her brow. Native

American female teachers still venerate Grandmother Moon and particularly highlight the dark moon, when the lunar face is hidden, a secret time to gather inner strength, and the full moon, the exact opposite, when her features are revealed in their fullness, looking outward with confidence.

As a woman, I find it wonderful to create a time of quiet at dark and full moon, just to focus inwardly and notice the subtle differences you feel within yourself. I tend to burn an incense blend indoors at dark moon, such as a pinch each of myrrh, lavender and marjoram to create a soft and very subtle aroma; at full moon I prefer to be outside, with more expansive aromas like a pinch each of jasmine flowers, frankincense and juniper berries. It is a very creative thing to work with your sense of smell and choose the ingredients you precisely want at a particular time.

Celebrating New Year

If you are like me, then New Year is something you dread—mainly because of the endless rounds of loud and unappetizing parties in so-called celebration. In recent years I have been glad to find others who want to do something a little more meaningful to mark the passage from one calendar year to the next. New Year is a time to digest and let go of the old and welcome the new, to release what holds you back and to create your intentions to move forward. I have been having aromatic fire-ceremonies for a few years now and they are greatly enjoyed by everyone. I mentioned this at the very beginning of the introduction, but here is the ceremony in more detail.

As well as preparing your aromatic fire as I describe in the previous chapter, you also need some pine cones, enough for each person to have one. As you get the fire ready, everyone should write down on a piece of paper something they want to release from the old year, in a phase starting 'I would like to release … because … '. When the coals are glowing, get people one by one to read out their statement, and then throw it onto the fire. When all this is done, then one by one each person can make a positive affirmation for the New Year, starting with 'I am … '. As they say their piece, they can throw their pine cone onto the fire and watch it burn. This is their prayer, their hope for the future, their statement of intent, a wonderful offering under a night sky. Native Americans call the stars the campfires of the ancestors— New Year is a marvellous time to work outdoors.

CHAPTER 6
SCENT AND SPIRIT

A S WELL as using incense in group situations where a celebration of some kind is happening, there is another level of personal work you can do with single ingredients which helps to deepen your own inner journey. This is an amazing exploration using your sense of smell, linked to just one plant type at a time, which allows you to explore where that particular aroma will take you. It also helps to teach you about individual fragrances and familiarise yourself with them, so this way of working is particularly advised for people who are starting out on their path with incense. Having said that, I often meditate with just one ingredient to remind myself of the signature, the individual profile of that particular plant, even after using incense and making it for several years.

I have selected ten of our incense ingredients, and for each one I am setting out some suggestions for a visualization. This simply means stilling and calming your mind, relaxing your body and allowing the aroma to take you on a journey, which I will describe so you can imagine it. Choose just one exercise to do at a time, prepare and perform the simple ritual and then give yourself time to absorb what your feelings tell you. You may like to keep a notebook to record feelings, draw impressions or write poems that may come to you.

Preparation for the exercise is simple. Tidy and clear a space, make sure the phone is off the hook and that you will be undisturbed. Prepare a table with a candle, some flowers and a glass of water to drink afterwards, as well as a mat on which to stand your incense pot. Then light a charcoal pellet outside, place it in your pot and bring it in, setting it beside the other items on the table. Sprinkle a pinch of your chosen ingredient onto the charcoal. Sit in a relaxed posture and gently inhale the aroma. Read the notes I have written as suggestions, then settle yourself, close your eyes and allow the fragrance to take you on your journey for five or ten minutes. When you are ready to come back to the room, stretch your arms and legs and take a few sips of water. Then immediately write down or draw your impressions.

You can record each exercise onto a tape to listen to if this is helpful.

You will see that I havegiven each ingredient a keyword or phrase to describe it. Allow your intuition to guide you to the one that feels right for you in the moment. Apart from rosemary, all other exercises can be done in the evening. Enjoy them.

Sandalwood—'grounding'

Inhale the woody, sweet aroma of pure sandalwood, sensing the rich hints of spice there in the smoke. Feel your body relax so you are comfortable and centred.

Imagine your spine is like the trunk of a tree, stretching upwards to heaven, and sending roots down deep into the earth. As you stretch your awareness upwards, your tree touches the stars. As you take your awareness downwards, you enter the realm of the mysterious kingdom of crystals, of the multi-coloured minerals that make up the earth. Use the rhythm of your breathing to travel up and down, slowly, and see if you feel a difference between 'above' and 'below'. Then as you continue to inhale the aroma, you can imagine sending strong roots down into the earth to hold and support you, to give your strength as you travel on through life.

Frankincense—'connecting'

Relax and enjoy the release of the pungent, richly warm aroma of pure frankincense grains burning. Breathe deeply and comfortably.

Imagine a night sky, darkest blue, velvety soft, scattered with diamond-bright stars.

As you look up, see the planets, stars, swirling constellations, the galaxies spread out all around you. Feel your feet firmly on the ground. Keep breathing the wonderful aroma; and as you look up, you will see one star that draws your attention. Keep concentrating on it, and it will grow larger as you look at it, as if you could see it through a telescope. How does your star look? What colour is it? Does it have rings around it? Is it very bright, or does its colour change? As you look at your star, it feels familiar; this is because it is your home in the heavens, it is your connection to the infinite Universe. You may feel it has a message for you. Listen carefully to the aroma, the key may be there.

Rosemary 'inner cleansing'

This is a good morning routine to try. Relax and inhale the lovely herbal aroma of rosemary, feel its pungent scent spreading all around you. Feel your feet on the ground and your body comfortable as you sit quietly.

Breathe slowly and comfortably, and as you do so take your awareness inside your body, as if you were carrying a torch which can shine throughout you, from your head, into your neck, your chest area, your back, your arms, your stomach, hips, down your legs to your feet. As you do this sweep, like a kind of 'inner scan', notice where there is any tension, any feeling of heaviness or discomfort, any areas that feel tired. Bring your awareness back up to your head, and repeat the scan, slowly; this time, when you reach an area that feels uncomfortable, inhale the rosemary aroma. Then imagine, as you breathe out, that the scent clears that place. Feel the tingling exhilaration which cleansing rosemary can bring. When you have done a second 'scan', relax and feel how your energy levels have changed.

Myrtle—'goddess'

The sharp and green aroma of myrtle with its hint of orange was considered by the ancient Greeks to be sacred to the goddess, the divine Feminine. Breathe in this aroma, and relax.

Imagine you are walking in nature, surrounded by flowers, colours, scents. The landscape will be familiar to you. Notice any features, such as hills, woods or water. You are content and happy in this place, the sun is warm, the breeze soft. As you walk, you see a female figure, and you greet her. Notice how she is dressed, and how she walks. She will address you, and you can ask her who she is. The goddess has many faces, many forms and many languages, but they all stem from the divine Mother, the feminine receptive principle. Ask for the grace to understand the goddess who speaks to you, and listen to her message. She may speak clearly, or she may give you something. Rest assured, she loves you very deeply. Whatever the message, its meaning will become clear to you.

European sage—'ancestors'

The deeply pungent aroma of sage is one of the most evocative incense aromas. Relax and inhale this wonderful rich fragrance.

Imagine you are sitting beside a wonderful campfire outside, maybe with a blanket over your shoulders, sometimes looking up at the night sky and sometimes at the wonderful gold, yellow and orange colour in the flames. It is a calm and peaceful night and there is no wind. As you sit, maybe looking through the flames, you realize that one or two others have joined you. Welcome them to your fire, and observe them. Maybe you know who they are, perhaps they are related to you, or maybe they are your guides, come to share the space with you. They may even be animals, come to share wisdom with you. Breathe the wonderful sage aroma and imagine you are talking to them and listening to what they have to tell you. Feel the companionship, the support and love of their presence. Remember to write down what they say....

Orange—'expansion'

The sharp and sweet aroma of burning orange peel spreads a soft and fresh fragrance all around you. Relax and inhale this lovely aroma.

Imagine you are standing in the middle of a field, whose boundaries you cannot see. It is warm and pleasant to be in such a space. Breathe deeply, and as you do so see if you can feel what you consider to be the boundary of yourself. Perhaps you consider that

to be your skin, for example. Breathe in the wonderful aroma of orange, and imagine that lovely fragrance fills the entire space you think is you. Keep breathing slowly, and see if you can really fill that space. Then, can you go further ... can you breathe so the essence spreads beyond what you think is your boundary? How does this feel? Don't push this, just go as far as you can. When you feel that is enough, then as you breathe draw the energy back into your frame, and into the core of your heart. Ancient wisdom teaches that we are much more extended beings than we believe. The more you practise this, the more you may find this out.

Lavender—'relaxation'

The aroma of purple lavender flowers burning is heady and sweet, a scent of summertime. Breathe in this gentle smoke and let your body rest comfortably.

Imagine a whole field of purple lavender flowers, as far as you can see. You walk through row upon row of blooms, and your eyes enjoy the contrast between the beautiful violet of the flowers and the silvery grey foliage. The flowers move to and fro in waves as the wind passes through them. As you breathe in the aromatic aroma of lavender as it burns, you let go of all anxiety and you rest, you are calm. No matter when you burn lavender, it brings with it the scent and heat of summer. It is a reminder of a time of light, and this is so valuable, especially in the depths of winter or when life brings challenges. Allow the vision of the soothing purple shade of the flowers, the heady scent and the light of the sun to bring you a sense of deep tranquillity.

Rose—'inner sweetness'

When rose petals fall on hot charcoal they release a highly intense and sweet aroma: one which is very swiftly gone, leaving only a subtle trace behind. If you 'listen' to this aroma, you may detect the remaining traces....

Place your hands over your heart and feel the warmth gather there. As you relax, breathe deeply and inhale the rosy scent of the petals in the burner, the sacrifice of the flower to the flame. Feel the aroma around you as you breathe deeply; imagine the colour and fragrance of the flower flowing into your heart. The lightness, the gentle quality of the bloom, surrounds you with peace and love. The petals are the offering of summer, the culmination of the plant's incredible work through the season to produce enough energy for a flower ... now released into the subtle realms. If you have something that you wish to dedicate, perhaps a new phase in your life, then express your intent for that new growth from this place of inner sweetness ... and trust that it will unfold.

Cardamom—'creative fire'

The warm and pungent aroma of cardamom burning is fiery and energizing. As you breathe deeply you feel a sense of growing vitality.

Imagine a candle flame burning; or, if you wish, concentrate on a real flame placed on a table before you. Breathe in the invigorating aroma of cardamom, and really focus on the flame. Notice its many colours, where it is brightest, where it is dimmest ... notice the subtle way in which it moves, it dances. Imagine that you could be inside the flame, moving and dancing with it, and that as you do, all doubts, fears and lack of confidence dissolve away in the power of the transforming fire. You are free, you dance the dance of your heart, you are restored and renewed. Feel the warmth of this creative fire spread through you, opening the realms of possibilities which you and only you can dream. Let this be a wonderful moving prayer for your life.

Benzoin—'new beginnings'

Granules of reddish benzoin gum release a lovely vanilla and cinnamon aroma, one which is sweet, warm and delicious. Relax and inhale this wonderful tropical fragrance.

Imagine you are going to create a door. This is going to be the most beautiful door you could possibly imagine. See it in absolute detail, in every way; what it is made of—wood, crystal, gold—what materials decorate it, like jewels, pearls, or even stars. Focus on this door and see how astonishing it is; and don't forget to include a handle—ornate, simple, bejewelled or plain, it does not matter. Add any symbols you would like to this door. When you have finished, see it as a complete thing; and yes, you have guessed, you do get to open it ... slowly and carefully or swiftly and exuberantly—just as you wish. Now where it is and where you are when you step through and where you will then be ... who knows? ... but may it be a place of magic, beauty, light and love, bathed in the fragrance of benzoin.

ENDNOTE

When the fire burns down, the embers still glow.
They carry the promise of a new fire, a new dawn.
They still hold a faint trace of the aroma of the sacred herbs.
Listen to that faint fragrance.
May your journey with incense be a source of inspiration to you
May you share it with others
And discover yourself.
Jennie

WITHDRAWN